Belonging

Belonging

ALUN WYN JONES

WITH TOM FORDYCE

Belonging

THE AUTOBIOGRAPHY

MACMILLAN

ISBN 978-1-5290-5808-6 HB
ISBN 978-1-5290-5809-3 TPB

135798642

A CIP catalogue record for this book is available from the British Library.

Typeset in Warnock Pro by Jouve (UK), Milton Keynes
Printed and bound by CPI Group (UK) Ltd, Croydon, CR0 4YY

MIX
Paper from
responsible sources
FSC® C116313